Louise P. Carroll

KINGFISHER

First published 2013 by Kingfisher
an imprint of Macmillan Children's Books
a division of Macmillan Publishers Limite
20 New Wharf Road, London N1 9RR
Basingstoke and Oxford
Associated companies throughout the wor
www.panmacmillan.com

Series editor: Heather Morris
Literacy consultant: Hilary Horton

ISBN: 978-0-7534-3319-5
Copyright © Macmillan Children's Books 2013

9 8 7 6 5 4 3 2 1
1TR/1012/WKT/UG/105MA

A CIP catalogue record for this book is available from
the British Library.

Printed in China

Picture credits

The Publisher would like to thank the following for permission to reproduce their material. Every care has
been taken to trace copyright holders. However, if there have been unintentional omissions or failure to trace
copyright holders, we apologize and will, if informed, endeavour to make corrections in any future edition.
Top = t; Bottom = b; Centre = c; Left = l; Right = r
Cover Shutterstock/Nikita Tiunov; 3 Shutterstock/Daniel Prudeck; 4-5 Getty/Superstock; 6–7 Shutterstock/
chantal de bruijne; 8 Shutterstock/Jasenka; 8–9 Getty/Corbis Bridge; 10-11 Shutterstock/Klayivik; 12 Alamy/
Imagebroker; 12-13 Shutterstock/Nikola Spasenoski; 14 Getty/Peter Arnold; 15 Naturepl/Kim Taylor;
16–17 Frank Lane Picture Agency (FLPA)/Horst Solliger/Imagebroker; 18–19 Getty/P&R Fotos; 20 FLPA/
Mark Moffet/Minden; 21 Getty/Phototake Science; 22 Getty/OSF; 23 Naturepl/Laurent Geslin; 24 Getty/OSF;
25 Specialist Stock/Cyril Ruoso/Bios; 26 Getty/Peter Arnold; 27 Getty/Bioshot; 28t Shutterstock/studiogi;
28b Getty/Martin Poole/The Image Bank; 29t Shutterstock/ George Filyagin; 29b Shutterstock/testbild;
30t Naturepl/Neil Bromhall; 30b FLPA/Mark Moffet/Minden; 31t Getty/Picture Press; 31b FLPA/Paul Hobson

Buzz!

What is that?

It is a bee.

Why does a bee buzz?

A bee is an **insect** with wings.

Its wings buzz when the bee flies.

4

This **honeybee** is busy.

She flies from flower
to flower.

She sips the flower's
nectar.

Munch, munch.

The bee chews the flower's **pollen**.

Pollen looks like a powder.

Some pollen sticks to the bee.

At the next flower, some pollen falls off the bee.

Seeds are made when flowers share pollen.

This busy bee helps new plants to grow.

And she doesn't even know it!

The honeybee flies home.

Her home is called a **hive**.

Many honeybees
share one hive.

13

Look!

The bee is still busy.

She wiggles.

She waggles.

The other bees watch.

What is she doing?

She is telling the other bees where to find food!

The hive is
a busy place.

Every bee
has a job.

The queen bee is the head bee.

She is the only honeybee
that lays eggs.

The queen bee is always in the hive.

She is the biggest bee.

Can you see her?

Worker bees take care of the queen.

They build rooms for her eggs too.

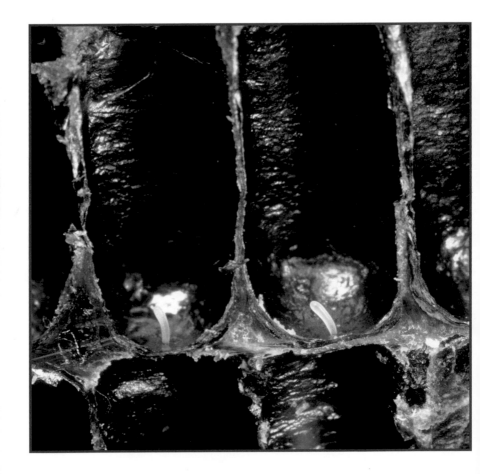

The rooms are made with
beeswax.

Honeybees make beeswax
inside their bodies.

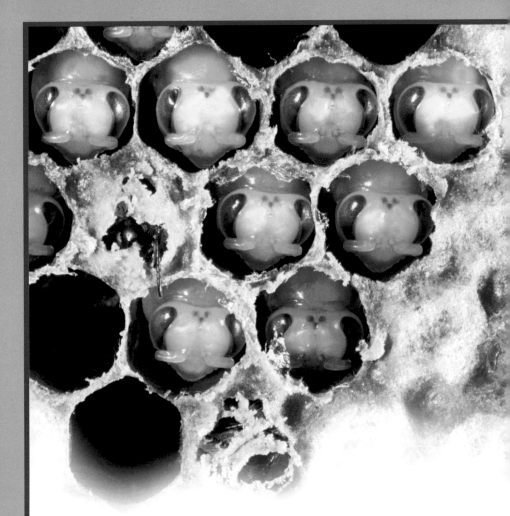

Each room has six sides.

Each room holds one egg.

The eggs **hatch** after three days.

But baby bees need
to keep growing.

Some worker bees
care for them
until they grow up.

Other worker bees
keep the hive safe.

They keep out bees and other
animals that do not belong.

They will sting
if they have to!

Some worker bees go
to get nectar.

They bring it back
for others to eat.

Honeybees save some nectar in the hive.

The nectar turns into **honey**.

The bees eat the honey.

We eat honey too.

It tastes sweet.

Do you
like honey?

We use beeswax too.

We use it
in crayons.

And we use it in candles.

Bees are busy!

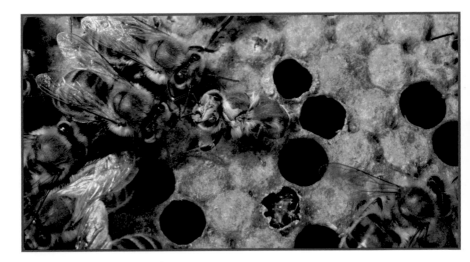

Some take care of baby bees.

Some bring food for other bees.

Some make honey and beeswax.

Bees help new plants grow too.

Buzz!

Glossary

beeswax the wax honeybees make to build rooms in their hive

hatch to break out of an egg and be born

hive a home that a group of honeybees live in

honey a sweet food that honeybees make from nectar

honeybee an insect that flies and makes honey

insect a small animal with six legs

nectar a sweet juice found in flowers that honeybees drink and use to make honey

pollen a powder found in flowers that is needed for seeds to be made and new plants to grow

seeds the small parts of a plant that will grow into new plants